ORVILLE, WILBUR & ME

MAGIC AT KITTY HAWK

BY

PHYLLIS R. MOSES

To Alyssa,

Try to fly higher, farther +
faster than ever before!

Phyllis Moses

5/04

ISBN: 1-4107-1918-9 (e-book)
ISBN: 1-4107-1919-7 (Paperback)
ISBN: 1-4107-1920-0 (Hardcover)

Library of Congress Control Number: 2003090651

This book is printed on acid free paper.

Printed in the United States of America
Bloomington, IN

Attribution:

Illustrations furnished by author
Photos courtesy of Outer Banks
Historical Society, Monteo, N.C.

1stBooks - rev. 06/20/03

ACKNOWLEDGMENTS

Few books are written alone. Writing a book is a collaborative effort. I owe a debt of gratitude to those who helped to make this book possible. Thanks to the many friends and colleagues who continually encouraged me.

To the people of Kitty Hawk, so generous with their information and advice about actual events: Especially to David Stick, Historian and Writer, and Bill Harris, the Mayor of Kitty Hawk, whose ancestors were original Kitty Hawk village residents.

I am profoundly grateful to those who wouldn't let me give up; family members whose faith in the project sustained me during these four years. I want especially to thank Ed Davis, fellow writer, dear friend and encourager; Richard Groux, Lorraine and Marvin Bruck who carefully edited the draft and made valuable suggestions; Myrna DuFord whose expertise with Microsoft Word program helped to format the document properly for publication.

My heartfelt thanks go to my family to whom I bestow my love of aviation history. I want to thank my husband, Brian Moses, for his patient, tireless re-reading and editing of the manuscript. Without him I would not have stuck to my guns. His persistent drive for clarity and simplicity was a constant irritant, but in the end, I knew he was right. Thank you, Brian, for keeping me steady on track. Your commitment to accuracy of the history and language of aviation, made the ingredients of the story come together seamlessly.

DEDICATION

To the late George E. Haddaway, whose vision of preserving the colorful history of aviation through the written word inspired and empowered this book. He mentored many aspiring writers and authors, urging us to respect, revere and record the past while looking forward to the bright future of aviation.

DISCLAIMER

"ORVILLE, WILBUR AND ME" is a book of fiction, based on historical facts. Although actual incidents used in this book have been told as accurately as possible, Joshua Morgan, Ezra Morgan, Nancy Morgan, their parents Etta May and Jim Morgan are entirely fictitious. Some of the scenes and situations did not actually happen. Many of the characters were patterned after local residents who lived in Kitty Hawk during the four years of trials, but the names used are fictitious. The heroes of the book, the Wright brothers, are legendary in the annals of aviation history.

AUTHOR'S PREFACE

There are many published books about the Wright brothers' famous first flight on December 17, 1903. However, the purpose of this book is to tell the story of the amazing miracle at Kitty Hawk, North Carolina, in language children of any age understand.

Winston Churchill once said, "Success is going from failure to failure without loss of enthusiasm." Those who make a difference don't always succeed the first time. The Wright brothers refused to let the almost insurmountable challenges change their objective.

Dorothea Brande said, "The Wright brothers flew through the smoke screen of impossibility." Indeed they did.

Bill Gates, CEO, Microsoft Corporation said, "The Wright brothers created the single greatest cultural force since the invention of writing. The airplane became the first World Wide Web, bringing people, languages, ideas, and values together."

Through this book, if one child's attitude about perseverance, hard work and tenacity is influenced, then it's a success. A secondary objective is to help children to establish dreams: dreams of exploring the possibilities, just as the Wright brothers did. Wilbur Wright said, *"I sometimes think that the desire to fly after the fashion of birds is an ideal handed down to us by our ancestors who, in their grueling travels across trackless lands in prehistoric times, looked enviously at the birds soaring freely through space, at full speed, above all obstacles, on the infinite highway of the air."*

To some people, the sky is the limit. To those who love aviation, the sky is home.

QUOTATIONS

"It's possible to make engines for flying, a man sitting in the midst thereof, by turning only about an instrument, which moves artificial wings made to beat the air, much after the fashion of a bird's flight."
~ Roger Bacon, 1220-1292

"When once you've tasted flight, you will forever walk the earth with your eyes turned skyward, for there you have been, and there you will always long to return.
~ Leonardo da Vinci

"The airplane has unveiled for us the true face of the earth."
~ Antoine de St-Exupery, "Wind, Sand and Stars"

"As soon as we left the ground, I knew I myself had to fly!"
~ Amelia Earhart, 1920

"To invent an airplane is nothing. To build one is something. To fly is everything!
~ Otto Lilienthal

"He rode upon a cherub, and did fly: yea, he did fly upon the wings of the wind." ~ Psalms XV111:10. The Old Testament

Wilbur Wright   *Orville Wright*

1900

CHAPTER 1

A Stranger Arrives in Kitty Hawk

Joshua Morgan balanced himself carefully on the slippery rocks at the edge of the water. Kitty Hawk Bay was quiet this time of the morning. There was hardly a ripple on the surface. The string he pulled along began to tug slightly. A crab was nibbling on a chicken neck tied to the line.

"Grab it," he murmured. About that time, the crab clutched the bait. Joshua carefully eased the line up, swung his net around and scooped up the prize. Josh chuckled, "There you go, big feller, right into my bucket."

The early morning sun rose higher over the bay. A strong breeze ruffled Josh's thick, reddish-blond hair. He was fifteen years old and a dreamer. Blue skies beckoned him, and birds in flight fascinated him.

Looking up, he saw a flock of seagulls flying about in the cloudless sky, diving and dipping into the waves to snatch their dinner from the water. As he watched, he thought, "I wish I had wings, then I could race around the sky like they do. The whole wide sky would be my world."

At Josh's side was his companion, Rascal, a mongrel dog that wandered into their yard years before. Rascal loved to go crabbing with Joshua. They made a good team.

Josh's younger brother, Ezra, 12 years-old, strutted back and forth on the pier nearby, pretending to be Blackbeard, the pirate who roamed the coast of North Carolina years before. His crude wooden

1

sword sliced swiftly through the air as his imaginary shipmates carried out his gruff commands.

"Hey, Ez, look here," Joshua called out to his brother, "my bucket's almost full. Ma'll be mighty happy." The crabs would make a fine feast. He reached down and scratched Rascal's ears. "We did a good job today, ole boy." Barefooted, he gingerly picked his way over the moss-covered rocks.

Something moving out in the bay caught his attention. Shading his eyes, he looked out across the water, spotting Mr. Perry's schooner anchored there. A skiff moved away from the larger boat and headed toward the shore.

As it neared the wharf, a man standing in the bow waved to them.
A feeling of curiosity stirred within Joshua, *"Who's this?"* he wondered. *"He looks funny, all dressed up fancy like a dude, even wearin' a derby hat."* Mr. Perry maneuvered his boat into the landing, shouting a greeting to the boys. Joshua leaned out and grabbed the side of the skiff as it came alongside. "Hey, there, Mr. Perry."

After the skiff was tied up, Joshua wiped his hands on his overalls, and then politely offered to help the passenger ashore. Ezra excitedly ran up and down the pier, tripping over his feet.

"Thanks, young man." The stranger said, grabbing Joshua's hand. "I'm Wilbur Wright."

"Mornin', sir. I'm Joshua Morgan. This here's my brother, Ezra, but we call him Ezzy. We live over yonder," he said, pointing to a house well back from the shoreline. "Can we help you with somethin'?"

"Yes, son, I believe you can. Tell me where I can find Mr. William Tate's home." He turned and waved his hand toward the cargo. "All of this here needs to be unloaded and taken there."

"Yessir, it ain't far, just over that ridge," Josh said, pointing to the south. "We'll load it on our cart and haul it over there. Ez, get the cart there from under the pier." His brother scrambled around and brought the cart up to the dock.

It was an unusually warm September morning. The sun beat down as they worked. By the time everything was unloaded from the skiff and reloaded onto the cart, all three were soaked with perspiration. Mr. Wright stopped a moment to wipe his face with his handkerchief. He removed his hat and fanned himself vigorously.

When the boxes, boards and bags were tied down securely, they moved away from the wharf, Joshua pushing and Mr. Wright pulling the rickety cart through the ankle-deep sand toward the ridge.

"Hey, Ez, take these crabs to the house and give them to Ma."

Ezra whined, "I want to come with you and help."

"All right, but make it quick. You can catch up to us."

As Ezra ran toward the house, he swung the crab bucket, sloshing water and seaweed along the way.

Mr. Wright and Joshua made their way down the sandy path "Josh, you're probably wondering why I came to Kitty Hawk. Well, I'm here to perform some tests." Wilbur Wright explained, "If everything goes well, these tests will prove a theory my brother, Orville, and I have."

Joshua stopped for a moment to wipe his flushed and sweating face on his sleeve.

"What's a 'thee-ree'? Is it like an idea?"

"That's close to being right, but it's really more than an idea - it's a scientific concept. We believe man can fly like birds."

3

At that startling statement, Joshua stumbled, almost falling. He looked at the visitor in astonishment. "Sir? What did you say, sir?"

Wilbur Wright chuckled, "You heard me right, son. We believe if a man has the right kind of machine, he can fly. If we don't run into any problems, I'll have a glider built by the time my brother arrives in a couple of weeks. Then we'll start our experiments."

"Golly!" Joshua exclaimed, "a flyin' machine right here in Kitty Hawk!"

"Yes, we plan to build and fly it here."

"Mr. Wilbur could I— I mean, may I—?" Joshua stuttered. His face flushed red with embarrassment.

"That's all right, Josh, you may call me Mr. Wilbur."

"Thanks, Mr. Wilbur. Is there anythin' I can do to help with your 'speriments? I'm 15 years old, and I'm strong as I can be."

"Why, I imagine there'll be plenty you can do, if it's all right with your folks."

The two new friends, totally unalike, walked along pushing and pulling the loaded cart through the deep sand. Wilbur Wright looked around curiously at the surroundings. He noted the tall sand dunes, the wide beach and the blue ocean beyond. Gazing about, he seemed pleased with everything he saw. Seagulls swooped above their heads, turned and dove, landing gracefully on the sandy beach.

Wilbur paused and watched the birds intently. Fanning himself with his hat as he rested, he murmured, "Yessir, this is a good and pleasant land, a perfect place for our glider tests."

CHAPTER 2

"YOU'RE GOING TO BUILD *WHAT?*"

Ezra skipped along the path through the dunes, oblivious to his surroundings. As usual, he was immersed in his fantasy role of Blackbeard the Pirate. As his imagination soared, a roguish smile spread across his freckled face. He gloated over treasures stolen from ships captured in the bay. His homemade sword sliced skillfully through the air, lopping off the heads of his hapless enemies.

Soon he caught up with the others as they neared the Tate's home. Rascal ran back and forth, nipping at everyone's heels, being a perfect nuisance. The Tate family came out to meet them.

"Howdy, Sir, you must be Wilbur Wright."

"Yes, I am, and you must be William Tate."

"Call me Bill, Mr. Wright."

"Wilbur," the visitor replied, offering his first name.

"Fine, fine," said Bill Tate.

With introductions out of the way, all pitched in to unload the cart, placing the odd assortment of bags, cartons and boxes on the front porch. At Tate's instruction, they stacked the long pieces of lumber by the side of the house. When they were finished unloading the cart, Wilbur Wright sat down on the porch, untied his shoes and emptied the sand out. As he did this, the Tate family sat down also and began to visit.

"Lan' sakes, Mr. Wright, what're you plannin' to do with all them long pine boards?" asked Mrs. Tate.

"Those will be the spars that go in the flying machine, ma'am. We wanted to use spruce, but the lumber yard in Elizabeth City didn't have spruce."

"Flyin' machine? All of this stuff is part of your flyin' machine?" Well, I guess you know what you're doin.'"

"You'll see," Wright smiled. "Just wait. You'll see."

Josh stood first on one foot, then the other, impatiently waiting for a polite way to take his leave. "We have to go home now. It's time for Pa to come in from the bay. He'll be lookin' for us to help him clean today's catch."

Wilbur gripped Josh's hand and patted Ezra's shaggy head. "Thank you for your help, boys, it was mighty nice of you to lend a hand."

Josh was embarrassed. Shyly, he stammered and shuffled his feet. "Aw, it ain't no trouble at all." With that, he jumped off the porch and beckoned to his brother.

"C'mon, Ez, I'll race ya' home."

The two boys sprinted off. They kicked up sand and hollered all the way home, with Rascal yapping at their heels.

"Ah, there you are, boys," Jim Morgan called out. "You're just in time to help me unload the fish." The boys, winded from all the running, took a moment to recover before they went to work. They quickly unloaded the fish from the wheelbarrow into the cleaning tubs.

Jim, a commercial fisherman, sold fresh fish to the families of Kitty Hawk Village, so each day's catch was important to the community and vital to the livelihood of the Morgan family.

As they worked, Josh told his father about the man he had met that morning. Jim listened intently. It wasn't often strangers came to the village.

"Yer Ma'll want to hear about this new feller comin' to our town. Soon as we finish cleanin' these fish, and settin' tomorrow's nets, you go tell her."

Josh nodded, hurrying with his work. Once finished, he headed toward the house. He leaped up on the porch and hastened into the kitchen. His mother was just putting away her work at the spinning wheel.

Etta May Morgan was a tall, soft-spoken woman who cared deeply for her family. Her auburn hair was pulled back loosely into a bun. She smiled with pride at her oldest child, reminding herself what a good boy he was.

"Supper'll be late tonight, Joshua. I've been spinnin' wool all afternoon."

"I'll help you, Ma, but just wait 'til you hear my news."

Etta May smiled as she reached up and gently smoothed the tousled hair that dropped into Josh's eyes.

As Josh helped his mother in the kitchen, his remarkable tale tumbled out. When he got to the part about building a flying machine, he became more and more animated, stuttering so badly his mother could hardly keep up with what he was saying.

Later at the supper table, Josh wanted to continue the story, but his father told him to wait until they finished eating.

And what a tasty supper it was! They dipped the crab meat in melted butter. Potatoes and onions were fresh from the garden. Dessert was a steaming blueberry cobbler. Supper over, they hurriedly cleared the round oak table, eager to hear Joshua's story.

8

Eight-year-old Nancy Adelia completed the Morgan family. Her bright red hair along with matching freckles set her apart. She didn't just come into a room, she exploded into it, with her bouncing energy and endless questions. Certainly, she was a joy to her parents, but always an aggravation to her brothers—at least, to hear them tell it.

Squeeker, the family's Calico cat, jumped up on Nancy's lap, demanding to be included in this important discussion.

As Joshua continued telling his story, Etta May and Jim exchanged disturbed glances that seemed to ask: "What kind of foolishness is this?"

Nancy, perched on the edge of her chair, was spellbound as Josh told them about Mr. Wilbur's plans for building the flying machine.

Everyone had questions: "Where is he goin' to build it?" asked Jim.

"How big will it be?" Etta May asked, skepticism plainly showing on her face.

Ezra wondered, "What will it be made of?"

"Mr. Wilbur and his brother plan to build their flyin' machine here in Kitty Hawk. He'll be putting up a work shed and a tent for sleepin', Joshua answered proudly. "He asked me to help."

At first, Josh thought his parents would be as thrilled as he was at the prospect of having the Wrights build an airplane here in this out-of-the-way place, but apparently they weren't. In his frustration, he wondered, *"Can't they see that somethin' real important is goin' to happen right here in our own back yard?"*

CHAPTER 3

The Morgan Family of Kitty Hawk Village

Kitty Hawk village is part of a peninsula that extends southward from the north end of the "Outer Banks."

Residents of Kitty Hawk and the Outer Banks had to be self-sufficient. Supplies and cargo could only be taken in by boat. Their isolation was complete.

The Morgan family lived off of the land. They owned two goats, a cow, and a garden large enough to produce all the vegetables and berries they could eat. The fruit trees were loaded down with peaches, apples and pears.

Delsey, their cow, furnished milk, cheese and occasionally, a calf. Two goats, Butty and Nipsy, ate everything in sight. They even ate the clothes off the clothesline if they got the chance.

Dan and Rhoda, the big sorrel and roan bays, pulled the plow, the wagon and the sled, but they were getting old and cranky. They no longer teamed up ready to go when they heard the rattle of the harnesses.

Fishing and hunting were excellent at Kitty Hawk, providing plenty of fish, ducks, geese, and venison for those who lived there.

Josh, Ezra and Nancy attended school where all grades studied in the same room. The boys chopped and stacked firewood in the woodbin for the coldest days. The girls cleaned the classroom. They also wiped down the blackboard each day, clapping the erasers outside to beat out chalk dust.

Few children attended school regularly. Most of the students were kept out of school from September to December to help with the seasonal fishing. There was always catching up to do in school.

Kitty Hawk Village had two churches: Baptist and Methodist. The Baptist church was "up the road"; the Methodist was "down the road," near the Morgan's house.

All the Morgan children were born in Kitty Hawk. Joshua had never been any farther than Elizabeth City, just across the Bay.

A life-guard station where a keeper and surf men manned the life saving equipment was located on the shore nearby. Because ships went aground in the shallows off shore, boatmen had to rescue many shipwrecked crews.

Another facility important to the Outer Banks was a U.S. Weather Station, which relayed warnings about gales, storms, and hurricanes, providing critical information for the local fishermen and mariners.

A lighthouse, white with black stripes painted from top to bottom in a spiral, was located at Cape Hatteras, a few miles farther south of Kitty Hawk. Its beacon continuously warned ships of the dangers of getting too close to the rocky shore. In years past, there had been so many tragic losses of ships hurled against the rocks, that this coast line was called "The Ship Graveyard."

When the Wright brothers were researching locations in which to test their flying machine, they sent out many inquiries across the country. In return, they received facts about climate, terrain, and weather patterns.

Bill Tate wrote to them, "This is a stretch of sandy land one mile by five with a bare hill in the center, eighty feet high, not a tree or a bush anywhere to break the evenness of the wind current."

They carefully evaluated each report. Eventually, Kitty Hawk, particularly Kill Devil Hills, became their final choice.

11

CHAPTER 4

THE VISION

The next day, Josh went over to the Tate's house to see what he could do for Mr. Wright. They were sitting out on the porch getting acquainted. As Josh walked up, Mrs. Tate said, "Howdy, Josh, come sit a spell."

He stepped up on the wide front porch and sat in the swing. "Thanks, Mrs. Tate."

Mr. Wilbur said, "Good day, Joshua, we were just talking about a likely place to set up our camp. Maybe you can go with me and we can look for one."

"Yes, sir, I'd be glad to do that. My chores are all done, so I have some time."

Mr. Wilbur and Josh stepped off the porch. Wilbur waved at the Tates, "I'll be back soon."

They walked along the cart path from the Tates' house down along the ridge. They talked about the Wrights' plans to build a flying machine here in Kitty Hawk. As they walked, Josh tried to match his stride to Wilbur Wright's, but finally gave up.

The two new friends found some driftwood to sit on while they talked.

Josh asked, "Mr. Wilbur how in the world did you and your brother get interested in buildin' a flying machine?"

Wilbur thought for a few minutes, and then said, "The desire to fly is as old as mankind, Josh. I guess our interest goes back to a toy that our father gave us when we were just small boys. It was only a stick with a four-blade rotor on top set in a hollow spindle. We held it in our hands, and when we pulled the string that was wrapped around the stick, the rotor rose out of the spindle and into the air. We wore it completely out. It was a fragile little thing, but we were fascinated with it. It lit a spark of curiosity in us that just burned brighter and brighter every day."

Josh asked, "When was this, Mr. Wilbur."

"Oh, I was about eleven years-old. Orv must have been seven. That small crude toy instilled the desire to read every book and paper we could find about the science of flying. We even got into trouble at school for fiddling with pieces of wood, trying to duplicate the toy. We made several of them, but when we tried to make larger ones, we failed."

"Soon after that, we built a crude kite with a 5-foot wing span, made of wood, wire and cloth. You know, Josh, all it takes for a dream to materialize, is to get that first spark. That spark comes from our imagination."

"Mr. Wilbur has anyone else that you know of had that same spark?" asked Josh.

"As a matter of fact, Joshua, two of the most inventive minds in the entire world spent many years trying to uncover the secrets of flight. One that we particularly studied was a German scientist, Otto Lilienthal. It was he who proved it was possible. He and his brother studied every detail of bird flight, making drawings and sketches of how their wings turned and curved. Tragically, he was killed in 1896 in an attempt to fly a powered craft he had designed and made."

Josh listened carefully to every word. Questions filled his mind, but he waited for Mr. Wilbur to speak again.

They got up from the make-shift bench and continued their walk. Mr. Wilbur continued, "Samuel Langley, an American, has been doing some credible work with different designs of flying machines in

Washington, but his efforts have not been successful. The U. S. War Department and the Smithsonian Institute have given him lots of money to develop his aircraft. My brother and I have read all the reports about his experiments of mechanical flight. We've studied every available book, paper and report on the subject. So we feel we're ready to design our own craft, and fly it."

Wilbur asked, "Josh, have you ever had a desire to fly?"

Josh answered, "Yes sir, I have. When I watch the birds around here, I wish I was one of them. They seem to be so happy and free. I guess that sounds silly, doesn't it?"

Wilbur said, "Not at all, Josh. Only a few have that dream. Undoubtedly, you are one of us."

About that time, they came upon a good place for the tent to be set up. They marked it with a piece of driftwood that had washed up on the sandy beach. Later, they went back and erected a tent for Wilbur and Orville to sleep in. This was also to serve as a kitchen and storage room.

That night, Wilbur wrote Orville to tell him about their new friends and their new temporary home.

CHAPTER 5

"JOSHUA, MEET MY BROTHER, ORVILLE"

It was September, 1900 scarcely two weeks following Wilbur's arrival. A heavy blanket of morning haze hovered over the bay. As the launch carrying Orville Wright neared the shore, shouts of greeting pierced the early morning air.

Orville leaped onto Kitty Hawk landing in one long step. The two brothers greeted each other with warmth and affection. Clasping hands, words tumbled out while they tried to catch up on the news. Josh could see they were exceptionally close. A bond of mutual respect was evident. Josh hadn't seen Wilbur this happy since he arrived two weeks ago.

The younger brother looked about, scanning the landscape to become familiar with the surroundings. He watched a hawk swoop, dive and then wheel back up into the sky.

"What do you think, Orv? Is it what you expected?"

Orville paused, continuing to look around him, "Yes, Wil, it's just as you described."

"Let me have your bag, Mr. Orville," Joshua offered.

Wilbur hastened to introduce them. "Oh, excuse me. Joshua, meet my brother, Orville."

"Glad to meet you, Mr. Orville."

"I'm pleased to meet you, Josh. My brother has written me about you and how much you have helped him."

15

"Oh, I ain't done much," Josh blushed and fidgeted, "I'm just glad to be of some help."

It seemed as if the whole town had gathered to watch. When the news spread that two bicycle mechanics from Dayton were going to build a flying machine, curiosity began to circulate about the community.

Wilbur had already earned a reputation for being eccentric. However, he was well respected for his gentlemanly manners and ways.

Orville had brought a large load of cargo with him. The ferryman helped by stacking boxes and cartons on the dock.

After a while, Wilbur smiled, "Orville, what all did you bring—the whole store?"

"In your letters, Wil, you said it was hard to buy coffee, tea and sugar here in Kitty Hawk, so I thought I would bring a supply. I know how you are about your coffee."

"Thanks, I *have* missed it a whole lot."

The cart creaked under the load. After some discussion, they decided to leave a few items on the dock for the time being.

Off they went to the Tate's home where they would stay until their camp was ready. Wilbur had already put up one tent at the camp site. Orville brought an additional one. Now they had sleeping quarters *and* a kitchen.

While waiting for Orville's arrival, Wilbur worked tirelessly on the glider. This additional time gave Wilbur a chance to talk to Joshua about their plans for the machine.

The two brothers were an odd couple. Wilbur, the elder of the two, often had a stern expression on his solemn face. But to those who knew him well, he exhibited a gentle dignity. His bulldog tenacity coupled with persistence carried him through many frustrating projects.

Orville, on the other hand, was sensitive and warm with a playful sense of humor. In spite of these differences, the two were more like twins, thinking the same thoughts, coming up with the same ideas.

They stopped their work often to watch the seagulls and hawks that were in constant view in the blue skies of Kitty Hawk. One day Wilbur explained to Josh about the dynamics of flight using birds in their flight as examples.

"Josh, watch that buzzard. See how hard it is for him to keep his balance? Now, that eagle up there just above the tree tops holds his wings level, so he has an easier time of it. The hawk flaps his wings harder and dives when he wants to go faster, or pick up thermals. Of course, they all flap their wings, but not like smaller birds."

"Do they use their tails?" Josh asked.

"Yes, they use them a lot, to help control their flight."

Wilbur had described to Josh how he and his brother planned to build a flying machine primarily as an experiment, and to apply some theories that would help to solve the problems of weight and balance. As Wilbur put it, "Once we get the machine under control in all circumstances, we can solve the motor problem."

Two weeks later, the brothers had the glider out on the beach, even though their anemometer measured the blowing winds at thirty-six miles an hour. Some days, ocean breezes were strong enough to allow them to work three or four hours at a time.

Phyllis R. Moses

Local residents were amazed at the goings-on of the brothers. They hid and watched from everywhere. Some stood on rooftops. Others watched from second story windows, or simply stood staring from the sand dunes.

Eventually, the Wrights decided to erect a derrick from which to attach ropes used to hold the glider. This way, they could fly it like a kite. But the glider wanted to rise higher, creating a major problem. When that happened, they pulled on the restraining ropes to maneuver it back down.

Wilbur and Orville explained to Josh that by doing this, they would gain knowledge about controlling the craft. Consequently, he began to understand the theory of lift. Many days were spent in the sand, flying kites, crashing them, doing it over and over again.

Gradually, the Wrights realized that the method of flying the glider from the derrick was flawed. Their disappointment was overwhelming. After many failed efforts they decided that their calculations were incorrect.

They had studied everything they could find of earlier experimenters' notes and practical applications. But from all the data they had read, nothing was working.

Usually, when supper was over, the two reviewed the efforts of the day. The young apprentice could see that the brothers were getting discouraged. Orville said, "It is one thing to fail, but still another because we don't understand why we failed."

One evening, Orville asked, "Could our numbers be wrong? There's bound to be something wrong with our theories about aerodynamics!"

"I've been wondering the same thing," Wilbur said. "I have an idea. Let's go back to basics. For now, we'll abandon the method of flying it from the derrick. We've tried that and it doesn't work. We'll fly it just like a kite, holding the ropes in our hands for control.

"I suggest we try gliding the machine from a higher dune. If we can do this, then we can leave Kitty Hawk feeling that we have given it our best effort."

CHAPTER 6

"WE'RE OFF!"

That night a nor'easter came roaring through the night. Any idea of flying the machine the next day was out of the question. The next two days were spent with the brothers holed up inside as sand whipped by the wind slammed into their tent.

When the storm abated, Josh came over to the camp. He found the Wrights digging the glider out of the sand. "Ho, Josh, you're just in time. We're going to higher ground to practice today. Will you please go fetch Bill Tate to help us carry the glider?"

With Tate's help, they carried it to the largest of the dunes. Finding just the right spot, Wilbur got into the glider and lay prone. Orville and Josh took one wingtip. Mr. Tate was on the opposite side. They moved forward slowly, just a foot above the surface of the sand. At that point, Wilbur hollered, "Let go." The glider eased forward, and then dropped slowly onto the sand, skidding along to a soft landing. With this modest success, Wilbur was ready for more.

Again, Tate, Joshua and Orville ran alongside, hanging on to the wingtips, then letting go so Wilbur could determine the function of the stabilizer and elevator. As he told them with great excitement, "I could feel just how far to move the controls in the face of the wind. This is it! This is what it's all about!"

Another glide brought even more knowledge of how the wings supported him and how the controls should be operated.

On the final glide of the day as the ground crew ran alongside in the sand, they realized they were picking up speed. Impossible to keep up with the craft, they let go of the wing as the glider began to lift. Wilbur, still well-balanced and maintaining speed, eased the glider back to the surface.

21

That evening in camp, everyone was jubilant. Wilbur told the crew, "We learned more today, I think, than from any other experiment. However, it's hard to call it a success when you realize that in all the glides put together, I've only had three total minutes in the air. Nevertheless, we're now more sure of the principles of flight."

Josh asked, "Will you be going home soon?"

Orville smiled slightly, sensing the concern in the question, "Yes, Josh. We must return to Dayton. There are problems to work out before we return next year. In the meantime write us now and then. We want to keep in touch."

Even though they were happy to be getting away from the brutal sun, sand and the primitive life here, the problems they had faced would keep them busy until they returned the following year.

CHAPTER 7

BACK TO THE DRAWING BOARD

The Wright brothers' first Kitty Hawk adventure was over. As they settled down to their old life in Dayton, Ohio the mysteries and magic of the time they spent on the Outer Banks of North Carolina continued to dominate their thoughts.

When they returned to Dayton, they found the bicycle shop in first-rate condition. Katharine and Lorin, their sister and brother, had managed it in their absence. A mechanic was hired to do bicycle repairs, enabling the brothers to work on their glider at home. The shop was their only income. It was their livelihood.

Since he was Joshua Morgan's self-appointed tutor, Wilbur decided to write him once a week. He felt it would encourage the new student's interest in the science of flying. Josh had become an important member of their crew.

Two weeks after their departure from Kitty Hawk, Bill Tate made a special trip to the Morgan's home to bring Josh a letter from Wilbur.

Joshua tore open the letter and began to read aloud:

> *"Josh, please share this letter with Bill Tate."* As Josh read this first line, he glanced over at Mr. Tate with a shy grin, *"We're home now and somewhat rested after our trip to your fair land. Many thanks for your warm hospitality and for the assistance that all of you gave to us during our experiments. We hope the blisters on your hands have healed up by now. We still spit out sand from time to time.*
>
> *"The problems with the glider still occupy most of our thoughts. We've made a decision to change the*

23

design. The control system is still a big puzzle. But of one thing we are certain, better control can be maintained through warping the wing. Unfortunately, at Kitty Hawk, we had neither the tools nor the materials to make these changes, so now we know we must work them out here before returning next season.

It's looking more and more like the calculations and graphs we've been using from earlier experimenters are incorrect. The time we must spend in determining new calculations and proving them is costly to us, but it must be done before we resume our work.

"We think it will be a good idea for you to study the notes we gave you about our experiments up to this point. In the meantime, Josh, be sure to watch the birds in flight as this will teach you more about flying than anything else."

"The exact date for our return trip is still indefinite, but we want to come long before the winter winds prevail. Again, thanks for your help and that of Mr. Tate."

Josh sighed as he folded the letter. "They have a lot of work to do, Mr. Tate. Flyin' that glider may look impossible to everyone else, but not to me. I know they'll figger things out."

CHAPTER 8

NOT EVERYONE LOVES A FLYING MACHINE

Although Josh had strong faith in the Wright brothers' dreams, Jim and Etta May Morgan were relieved when the Wrights went home. Not only had their son spent every waking minute with them, but he had also begun to act strangely. He was still a good son, but he seemed to be in a dream world, distracted by the activities of "those crazy Wright boys."

Etta May mused, "Jim, should we help Joshua with his school work more? He's always been good at math and science. Maybe with more encouragement he'll look for other ways to find excitement, and he'll finally see those Wright brothers for what they are: just rich playboys that have nothin' better to do. What do you think?"

"Etta May, our Josh is going to be all right. This is a new adventure for him—just the way Ezra is always play-acting like Blackbeard, the Pirate."

Jim's voice became tender as he reached over to pat his wife's hand, "He'll change. We don't want to make too much out of it, for then he might rebel and make things worse.

"Besides, have you noticed the way he's studyin' more of late? He goes to see Mr. Dosher over at the Weather Station to talk about weather, and he's always readin' the papers the Wrights wrote about buildin' that machine. One good thing about all this: he seems to have a new interest in those subjects."

Etta May sighed, folded her handwork and placed it in her sewing basket. She stretched as she rose from her chair, realizing she had been sitting there for over an hour.

Squeeker, the cat also rose and stretched. He arched his back and yawned. Jim reached over and scratched him behind his ears.

"Etta May," he chuckled, "We have a fat, spoiled cat, here."

"I think you're right, Jim. He's too lazy to even chase mice any more. Oh, look at the clock. I must get supper started. The Tate's are comin' over this evenin' for a visit. Mrs. Tate's made her girls some Sunday-go-to-meetin' dresses out of that sateen material those boys used on the wings of that infernal flyin' machine. She's goin' to bring 'em along to show us. She said she might have enough left over to make our Nancy one."

Jim walked over to the window and parted the curtain. "Where are the kids, Etta May? Shouldn't they be in by now?"

"I 'spect they're down by the water's edge, looking for shells and treasures. They'll be along soon enough, when they get hungry."

Jim went out the screen door to the wide porch that ran the entire front and side of the house. About that time, he heard the children's whoopin' and hollerin' as they made their way home. Nancy ran ahead of the two boys screaming her lungs out. They were teasing her, saying they were going to throw her in the bay. When she saw her father, she ran headlong into his arms, breathless and shuddering with dread that they might still catch her.

"Slow down, you wild injuns, leave this young'un alone. You've scared her plumb out of her wits!" As the boys reached the porch everyone joined in the fray. Etta May listened at the kitchen window. She smiled contentedly at the antics of her family. All was well with the Morgan family tonight.

CHAPTER 9

A LETTER FROM DAYTON

Supper in the Morgan household was family time. After they had finished their meal, Joshua told about his letter from Mr. Wilbur. Ezra and Nancy pleaded: "Read it, Josh. Read it out loud to us."

With this bit of encouragement, he pulled the letter out of his pocket and began to read. As he read, his mother frowned and glanced at her husband, who was listening intently to their son.

After Josh was finished, Jim said, "Sounds like those boys intend for you to be helpin' in the 'speriments on that flyin' machine."

"Pa, I want to help, if I can. I'm strong enough to help carry the machine to the hills for the takeoffs. They seem to trust me with some of their ideas, and I know Kitty Hawk better than they do."

"I know you want to help 'em," his mother said quietly. "That's mighty big of you, but shouldn't you be studyin' your three R's?"

"Ma, I'll be learnin' more'n my three R's next year. The brothers would kinda' like for me to take up the science of flyin' in my studies."

"Well, how in the name of sense can you do that here in the country school of Kitty Hawk?" asked his Mother.

"I'm goin' to be studyin' their airplane-makin' books. They have a ton of 'em. And I 'spose they'll help me with the hard parts."

Jim threw Etta May a warning look as if to say, "That's enough, for now."

"Son, if you're this interested in them flyin' machines, then we need to be thinking about what you'll have to do after you finish high school. You'll need some more schoolin'. Much as I want to help you, how can a poor fisherman like me afford such as that?"

Josh walked to the window and looked out, trying to hide his disappointment. He dropped his head in discouragement. Just then Jim came over and gave him a big bear-hug. They both looked embarrassed. He whispered to Josh, "We'll work this out someway, son."

"Thanks Pa."

When the kitchen was tidied up, the family was ready for company. Bill Tate was considered the best-educated and most knowledgeable man in the Village. Not only was he commissioner of Currituck County and a Notary Public, but also the local Postmaster.

Mrs. Tate was resourceful—as all the women of Kitty Hawk Village had to be. Being a good neighbor, she took care of people when they were sick or needed help. She and Etta May had become good friends.

When the Tate family arrived, the Morgans met them on the front porch. The children soon scattered to play outside, giving Etta May a perfect opportunity to discuss her concerns.

"Let's go into the parlor where we can be more comfortable. Now, Mr. Tate, you and Mrs. Tate know the Wright brothers better than most of us, you've had 'em in your home. What do you think of 'em?"

Mr. Tate glanced at Etta May and lit his pipe. "If you're worried about their character or their intentions, you needn't be. They paid me good for room and board, and treated my wife and kids with respect. Is somethin' botherin' you, Mrs. Morgan?"

"I guess I'm just curious about 'em, that's all. There are lots of things that ain't quite right. For one, why ain't they married, at their age?"

"Well, Mrs. Morgan, I wondered the same thing, then one day Wilbur told me their main goal was to build a flyin' machine And like he said, 'we can't support wives and support a flyin' machine too.' One thing that impressed me and my missus here is their faithfulness to honor the Sabbath Day. I don't know if you've noticed, but they don't do their experiments on Sunday."

"Why is that, Mr. Tate?" asked Mrs. Morgan.

"Main reason is, because their father is a Bishop in the church, and they respect him too much to disregard his wishes. For this I commend them."

About that time, Josh and Tommy Tate returned to the living room. "Got any more gooseberry pie, Ma?" asked Josh.

"Sure, you boys just help yourselves to pie there in the kitchen. Did you see the girls? Where are they?"

"Aw, they're just chasing lightning bugs in the yard right now."

Mrs. Tate brought the dresses she had sewn out of the wing material to show Mrs. Morgan. Mrs. Tate told how she went out to the glider the Wrights had abandoned in the sand that fall, and with her scissors cut the material away from the wood. After she washed the material carefully, she pressed it with her smoothing iron. It was perfect for the girl's dresses. Since there was some left over, she suggested they make a dress for Nancy. Etta May accepted her offer with gratitude.

After the Tate's left, Jim and Etta May sat in the rocking chairs on the cool side porch.

A kerosene lantern provided a soft light. Etta May had her ever-present sewing basket with her; her lap was filled with socks to be darned. Again, she brought up the subject about Josh and the Wright brothers.

She began, "Jim, please listen to me, I'm concerned about. . . ."

Jim interrupted his wife, putting his large calloused hand over hers, saying, "Etta May, I want to ask you somethin': Would you be happier if Joshua never had a chance to do better for himself than he'll find here in this backwater village?"

"You know I don't mean anythin' like that. But I don't see this is as a great opportunity for Joshua. They haven't really proved anything yet. How many years will it be before they find out if that machine will actually fly? Even then, is there a proper place for our son in their plans?"

As Jim puffed on his pipe, he replied, "I wish I could answer your questions, darlin' but some things just need to work out for themselves. The brothers are smart, there's no doubt about that. They're determined and they're honorable. So, all I can say is that we should just trust for the rest of the story."

Jim's pipe smoke drifted lazily around his head as he rocked back and forth. He glanced over at his wife. She still looked troubled.

Jim cleared his throat and spoke again, "Darlin, I understand the Wrights are coming back to Kitty Hawk about the eighth or tenth of July. That's just around the corner. Don't you think we should show Joshua we trust him by letting him help the Wrights? We see him as our little boy, but he's almost a grown-up man, and it's time for us to give him a little slack."

She sighed and rose from her chair, "Very well, Jim I'll hush. Maybe not for good, but I will try be more understandin.'" She twisted the loose strands of hair back into the bun at the nape of her neck, and then absent-mindedly brushed her apron down smoothly.

"I'll try. I promise I'll try."

1901

CHAPTER 10

THE WRIGHT BROTHERS RETURN TO KITTY HAWK

The Wrights arrived back in Kitty Hawk in the summer of 1901 in the midst of one of the worst storms they had ever experienced. But, after the storm abated, it didn't take long to erect their tents and buildings.

Josh helped build shelves, and put away their supplies. After that, they built the world's first airplane hangar to house the new glider. Right away they got to work on the machine, which was considerably larger than the 1900 glider. Its wing surfaces had an area of 290 square feet, as opposed to 165 square feet of last year's plane. Josh nicknamed it "The Whopper." The name stuck.

Josh was there, as usual, to help get everything set up for the glides. They dragged the new glider about half-way up Kill Devil Hill where they would try again to move the craft forward into the air. It was a frustrating experience because they were constantly battling the wind and blowing sand.

After several attempts to fly the new glider, the results were grim. It kept falling back into the sand. However, on the tenth try, the glider flew into the gentle wind. Everyone watched in amazement when the machine rose higher and higher.

The excited ground crew shouted for Wilbur to get the plane under control.

Orville yelled as he ran along the track, "Wil, shift your weight. Get the nose down a little, or it'll stall."

Wilbur shifted his weight on the bottom wing. The machine descended gently then settled back into the sand.

33

Everyone crowded around Wil as he came off the wing, congratulating him on the small success of the morning.

For the rest of the day, the pilots and their support crew made several more attempts.

That night, as he often did after a tiring day, Orville picked up his mandolin, strumming away while Wilbur and Josh sang along with the music. Though they were often exhausted, it was a good time to review events of the day. Wilbur said, "Even though the same conditions exist we experienced last year, we've now learned more about how to control the horizontal stabilizer. But even having this new knowledge, there are still some missing pieces."

Joshua pondered this, but he was unable to fully understand the brothers' dilemma. Still he wished he could come up with some good facts that might help solve the glider's problems.

He was eager to learn more. The time he spent helping with the experiments flew by. Whether he was holding onto a wing or running back and forth through the sand, he never tired of his task. He felt a thrill each time he watched the glider go even farther, lifted by the wind and controlled by the pilot.

1902 GLIDER

CHAPTER 11

IF AT FIRST YOU DON'T SUCCEED

August 9th was a crucial day in the lives of the Kitty Hawk fliers. The crew once again carried the glider up to the peak of the great sand dune, Kill Devil Hill. There were many flights that day. On the whole, Wilbur felt satisfied with the results. He said, "I really feel like I'm beginning to understand what's happening. What I don't understand is why the machine doesn't respond to manual changes of the controls. Each time we start a turn a wingtip dips into the ground."

By the middle of August, Orville and Wilbur realized the glider's problems were far more serious than they had originally thought. With this disappointing realization, they packed up their possessions and headed home. They would try to work out the solution in their workshop.

On the long train ride to Dayton, the unhappy pair agreed that when they considered the time and money spent in trying to prove their theory that man could fly, they had begun to doubt they would ever solve their problems. Feelings of despondency and utter failure overwhelmed them.

Wilbur said, "If the day should come when man will fly, it will not be in our lifetime, or within a thousand years."

This dismal prediction would be contradicted in just two more years by the very man who spoke those words that day.

With what slim threads was the future of aviation tied!

CHAPTER 12

AT HOME IN DAYTON

Seeing the brothers' faces, it was apparent to Katharine they needed more than just physical rest. When they arrived back home, they couldn't talk about their recent experiences at Kitty Hawk. Their spirits were badly broken.

Katharine told them, "Remember, you are challenging unknown factors: "There are barriers up in the sky – barriers you must overcome."

With this bit of insight from their sister, they began to look at the situation from a different perspective. Gradually, they moved out of their black cloud of gloom.

When Wilbur wrote to Josh, telling him about the progress made on their revised tables, graphs and calculations, he began to understand. Often, he visited Mr. Dosher at the Weather Station to seek his help in understanding the more difficult problems.

In one particular letter, Joshua read,

> *"We think we're building a glider that contains improvements we learned in our two previous seasons at Kitty Hawk. Our calculations call for a slightly larger machine than the one we had last season. It will have a wing area of 305 square feet We've been doing wind tunnel tests in order to select the most efficient airfoil shape."*

Joshua read the letter and began to visualize the new glider with more wing span, up to ten feet longer. In his spare time, he made drawings of the gliders they had brought to Kitty Hawk up to now. The new glider was significantly improved over earlier ones.

As time drew near for the brother's third trip to the testing grounds, they spent a lot of extra time marking, cutting and sewing fabric for the wing coverings. Finally, they were ready to return to Kitty Hawk.

CHAPTER 13

THE MAGIC OF KITTY HAWK

Josh was still out of school for the summer when the Wrights came back to Kitty Hawk. He and Ezra met them at the wharf. Of course, Rascal was also eager to see them.

As the launch brought them alongside, greetings seemed louder than usual. There was a new excitement in the air. The Morgan boys had grown a lot over the summer. Josh was now quite a tall young man, so was Ezra.

Additional carts were brought in to transport the supplies to the campsite, which had to be dug out of the sand drifts collected around the doors and windows.

On the afternoon of September 8th, the work on the new glider began. Calculations of lift and drag were carefully reviewed.

"Josh, with your help we can fit these wings onto the glider. We're anxious to take it out and see how it performs for us." When the glider with all the new changes was taken out for trials, it made over fifty runs by late September.

Wil's progress in the following two weeks in the machine was remarkable. He could fly it straight ahead or make it stand still in the wind. Orville, however, eased into the learning process gradually. Knowing he must first get acquainted with the controls, he began by performing short glides.

Typical East Coast weather prevailed that fall. There were torrential rains with high winds, or no wind at all. By October 2, they had flown as much as twenty-five times a day, achieving distances of 500 feet and more. The long winter studies with the wind tunnel had begun to pay off.

The fixed rudder was still a problem with the 1902 glider. After many sleepless nights, Orville had an idea. As he thought through the various problems they had experienced, a possible solution came to him. Why not hinge the rudder, making it a double vertical fin? The more he thought about it, the more sense it made. He could hardly wait until morning to tell Wil about it.

At breakfast, he explained his ideas about the rudder to Wil. After serious thought, Wil agreed the idea had merit. They made sketches. They argued the pros and cons, and then they went to work on the new design.

On October 10, Wilbur took up the glider with the new rudder. It certainly was more manageable. Again and again they took it up, with favorable results.

It was now safe to say that the redesigned 1902 glider proved they had solved the problems of flight control.

Josh was spending more time helping the brothers out on the dunes. His parents, while not openly opposing him, tried to fill his time with what they called, "more important things." However, the demands of the project were increasing. Josh was torn between his duty to his parents and his participation in the Wright brothers' project.

Most Kitty Hawk residents were still skeptical of all this "foolishness." Josh was puzzled by their attitudes, not only from his family, but other residents as well. He believed the Wright brothers were developing something that would make a huge change for the world.

The people of Kitty Hawk considered Josh, (now 17 years old), still "wet behind the ears." The fact that he was helping two eccentric men fly their kites was the subject of many interesting discussions.

Josh kept a diary detailing the progress of their experiments. In his entry for October 28, 1902 he wrote:

> *"So far this year, the brothers have made over 250 glides. The handling of the machine is greatly improved. Mr. Wilbur set a record of a single glide covering 622.5 feet in just 26 seconds. I think they are about ready to put an engine on the glider, since most of the problems of control and wing warping have been worked out."*

When the time came for the Wrights to go home, they were thrilled over their success. They would have liked to do additional glides, but members of the crew needed to get back to their seasonal fishing, and Josh had to go back to school. They broke camp October 28th and headed home to Dayton.

CHAPTER 14

FINDING THE RIGHT POWER PLANT

In a letter Josh received after their return to Dayton, Wilbur described the frustration of trying to find the correct engine for their glider:

> *"I wrote to ten manufacturers of engines, inquiring about prices and delivery for a gasoline engine that would weigh no more than 180 pounds and deliver eight to nine horsepower. However, there were absolutely no responses at all to my inquiries. Therefore, our mechanic, Charlie Taylor has agreed to build one for us. Even now, he has begun to work on it, and it's coming along quite well. We're also exploring ideas for the propeller. We hope to have the answers on this by next March."*

Predictably, the engine proved to be a challenge. It was cranked up for its first test-run on February 12, 1903. It was crude, yet everyone agreed it had definite possibilities.

Meanwhile back in Kitty Hawk, Josh kept a diary and a scrap book, including letters he received from Mr. Wilbur. Impatiently, he counted the days until their return to his village.

Because there were delays in preparing the new engine for shipping, it was not until September when the brothers finally set out to Kitty Hawk.

As usual, Joshua met them at the landing. It took a couple of days to repair damage the storms had done to their shed, but with Mr. Tate, Joshua, Orville and Wilbur doing the work, it went faster than expected. A second hangar was built to house the new aircraft and engine.

The time had now come for the first powered flight attempt. Unfortunately, it didn't go as planned. The sprockets resisted any effort to be tightened. The magneto failed to develop a strong enough spark to run the engine.

Josh told the story at the supper table that night. "There we were all ready to go. Then we couldn't get it off the ground!"

His father asked, "What happens now?" Josh shook his head, "They had to send the propeller shafts and the magneto back to Dayton for Mr. Taylor to repair."

While the Wright brothers waited for the repaired parts to be returned from Dayton, they spent hours endlessly going over calculations. Josh soaked up the technical data, writing it down in his journal, learning as much as he could about the science of flying.

A hundred years ago, residents of small towns like Kitty Hawk, through economics and inaccessibility, often abandoned hopes of higher education. With Josh's new interest in aviation, his parents were faced with a new reality: Josh must have more education.

A search for just the right college yielded several choices. The University of North Carolina was the most logical. It was closer to Kitty Hawk than some of the others, and Josh's grades were more in line with the entrance requirements.

Tuition was a big factor in choosing a school. With Wilbur's help, Josh applied for a 4-year scholarship to cover all his expenses. Naturally, he was impatient to hear the results of his application, but with all his chores, plus the demands of his senior year in school, time flew by.

CHAPTER 15

"GETTING IT RIGHT"

To facilitate a successful takeoff of the flying machine, the Wrights built a sixty-foot horizontal launching rail. It was soon nick-named, "The Grand Junction Railroad," because the airplane would ride on two bicycle wheel hubs the length of the rails before it took off.

More problems with the propeller shafts caused additional delays. Orville took them back to Dayton a second time for repairs. In the meantime, Wilbur coached Josh on his college entrance exams. But there was also plenty of work to do at the camp. They pulled up stumps, cut wood, and did many things to stay busy.

Orville returned to Kitty Hawk in mid-December with the newly repaired propellers. It took only one day to reassemble the aircraft. When it appeared they were ready to leave for the dunes, Wilbur suddenly had an idea. He said, "Josh, let's hoist a red banner on the side of the hangar. It will signal the boys down at the life saving station we are going to attempt another flight and we'll need their help."

The excitement in the Wright camp grew, especially when local men and boys began to gather in response to the signal.

"Let's go, boys! This is it! Today is the day we're going to fly this machine," exclaimed an excited Orville.

It was back-breaking work moving the 700-pound glider to the right spot for the launch. By mid-afternoon the machine was securely fastened to the end of the rail. When the brothers started the engine, the thunderous clatter and roar sent some of the on-lookers scrambling to get away from the noise.

During the engine's warm-up, Orville and Wilbur took a moment to toss a coin, a method they had previously agreed on to decide which one would pilot the plane on its first flight.

Wilbur won the toss. He quickly clambered aboard the wing and assumed a prone position. After checking the controls, he signaled for the crew to push the machine. It moved forward. However, it went too fast for them to keep up, causing it to rise into the air and nose up sharply. Slowing down, it fell back into the sand. The resulting crash did some damage, but did not injure Wilbur.

The date was December 16th. All that day and the next morning, they worked on the damaged craft.

By the time they had finished with the repairs, the weather had changed. It was not good for flying. But the patience and hope ever-present in Wilbur's attitude encouraged everyone to look forward to tomorrow, when they would make another try.

1903

CHAPTER 16

SUCCESS, AT LAST

December 17th dawned cold and clear. After breakfast, the brothers re-hung the banner to signal everyone to come and help. Orville and Wilbur were dressed, as usual, in suits, white shirts with starched collars and ties.

Josh got up early to tend to his chores before going over to the Wright's camp. Jim Morgan agreed to allow Josh to miss school for this big day.

Josh trotted over to the camp. By the time he arrived, several crewmen had come to help with the launch. This was going to be an important occasion. How important, they had no idea!

Under the Wright's supervision, the helpers again lifted the heavy glider and carried it to Kill Devil Hill. The rails were re-positioned in the sand. All controls, wires and connections had to be checked, and everyone was briefed on their individual duties.

When the Wrights were certain all was ready, the countdown began. Spectators had gathered on the beach of the island. It seemed the entire village was present. There were skeptics, disbelievers and those who had ridiculed the brothers. But most of them had come to admire the two men for their persistence and determination.

By 10:30 that morning, everything had been checked. At last, they were ready.

CHAPTER 17

FLIGHT

The brothers made many efforts that morning to launch the flying machine. It was almost noon when they decided to make one more attempt before they broke for lunch.

Orville got into the pilot position atop the wing. He started the engine, checked the instruments, and looked to be sure no one was around the wings. When he was certain everything was set, he gave the signal and released the restraining wire.

After a brief hesitation, the aircraft moved down the rail, and rose into the air. As it became evident Orville could maintain control of the craft, Josh went racing across the sand dunes, waving his arms and shouting, "WE'VE DONE IT! WE'RE FLYING!

A shout went up. Onlookers clapped, jumped up and down and loudly cheered.

"Did you see it?" Josh asked, "Our airplane took off under its own power, and landed. Right here in Kitty Hawk, a man flew an airplane. I knew they could do it. Didn't I tell you they would? I knew it all along."

Orville's official time and distance for that first flight was 120 feet in twelve seconds.

Many other successful flights were made that day. The best flight was when Wilbur took off and flew 852 feet in 59 seconds, their best time and distance for the entire day. This became the official time and distance for the record books.

It was an excited crew that returned to camp that day. Past failures and disappointments were forgotten. Plans for a new, improved

Wright Flyer were discussed. The brothers had achieved success at last.

CHAPTER 18

GOING HOME AGAIN

For the next four days, Josh helped the Wrights break down the camp and collect all their belongings. They packed the aircraft into boxes and barrels for shipment. The intense pressure that had hung over them for so long was gone now. The three had time to relax and talk about the future.

Wilbur asked, "Josh, would you like to remain a part of our team? We can't promise you much at this point, but we plan to build another aircraft to replace this one. With your first hand knowledge of our design, and your up-coming engineering studies, you can come into the Wright Airplane Company as our first design engineer. What do you think?"

Josh was overwhelmed with the confidence they placed in him. His face flushed with pride, and his lips quivered as he heard those words from his friend, Wilbur. To cover his embarrassment, he turned away and dug the toe of his boot into the dirt floor of the tent.

He had been their principal crew member for four seasons. It had been a delicate balance, trying to be available to help them, even at the risk of angering his parents. The Wright's vision became his vision, and he never let go of it.

"Thank you, Mr. Wilbur and Mr. Orville. I dunno' know what to say. Thanks for your confidence in me. I've dreamed of going to work for you since you first came here," said Josh, "but I never thought it would be possible, not in a million years."

"I have to talk to my parents about this first. I'll give you my answer soon."

"Certainly, Josh. You're a fine young man. We've discussed this between the two of us, and we're certain you would be a big help to us," said Wilbur. "But it's very important that your parents feel the same way about this as we do. So discuss it with them, and then let us know what you all decide."

1904

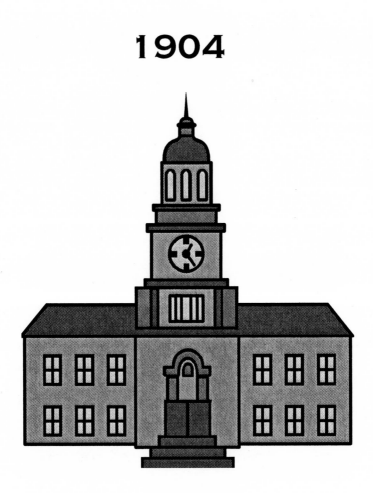

CHAPTER 19

OFF TO SCHOOL

While the Wright brothers were settling back down to a nearly normal life in Ohio, the residents of Kitty Hawk were basking in their newly found celebrity status. Their historic claim to fame was that the first powered flight was performed right here on this narrow spit of land.

Jim and Etta May Morgan were quite surprised to learn about the successful flight, being doubters from the beginning. They had often wondered, "What do two bicycle mechanics know about buildin' airplanes?"

Josh approached his Mom and Dad about his future plans. His application for a scholarship had been accepted, which cleared the way about the financing. So after much discussion, they finally agreed his arguments had merit. Plans were made for him to enter the University upon graduation from high school.

When a course of studies was being selected, the subject of aviation engineering was non-existent. However, there were other engineering courses open to him that would lay a solid foundation for him to become an aircraft engineer.

Josh worked hard on his college courses, making good grades. Even though he was not an outstanding student, his progress was good enough to warrant the renewal of the scholarship funds each year.

During his holiday breaks and summers, Josh spent time in Dayton, **hel**ping the Wright boys build the next generation Wright Flyer.

By the time he graduated from the university, Josh was equipped with a good basis of mechanical engineering and the science of flying. The vision of building airplanes with the Wright brothers burned brighter than ever in his dreams.

CHAPTER 20

THE WRIGHT AIRPLANE COMPANY

When the Wright brothers returned to Dayton, there was hardly any recognition or attention paid to their miraculous achievements at Kitty Hawk. Messages they sent by wire announcing the successful first powered flight were either not published in the newspapers, or were misquoted. There was no fanfare.

However, members of their family, Katharine, Lorin, Reuchlin, Bishop Wright and their housekeeper, Carrie, greeted them with beaming pride. The brothers had not eaten properly for several weeks, so the first order of the day was to have a victory meal.

The conversation was lively at the dinner table. The family's encouragement and support during these four years had been their principal source of strength. Now there was no question about it, the proof of the first flight under power was indisputable.

Eventually, the conversation turned to those who helped at Kitty Hawk. When Josh's name came up, Katharine said, "If this young man is as bright as you say he is, then he should be put to work here on future projects."

"Katharine, you are right. Josh was our strongest supporter on the project," answered Wilbur. "He risked his schooling, as well as his parents' anger in spending so much time helping us. We might have been able to do it without him, but I wouldn't have wanted to try."

"Another admirable trait about Josh: he stood out there on the coldest days, shivering and blue, hanging on to the wing tip of that glider," interjected Orville, "And he never complained. He was as persistent as we were."

Bishop Wright said, "I understand you offered him an opportunity to work with you here in Dayton. Is that true?"

"Yes, father, we did," Orville replied. "Josh is now enrolled in the University of North Carolina. He has agreed to work for us in the summertime and during holiday breaks, until he graduates as an engineer. We'll get him here one way or another."

Although Orville and Wilbur immediately began to build their next Wright Flyer, they made time to write to Joshua weekly detailing their projects. In one of Wilbur's letters, he wrote:

> *"We have found a location for our flying tests. It's called Huffman Prairie, eight miles outside the city. We are building a shed to house our glider, and even though the property is bordered by trees, poles and power lines and an occasional cow wandering about, it's free for us to use.*

The new Wright Flyer was almost ready for testing. About fifty news reporters and magazine journalists were invited to attend. However, many unfavorable conditions cropped up to cause the entire exhibition to be a failure. The guest journalists took advantage of these failures to ridicule the Wright brothers in the press.

Although some small success was achieved that year for the two "Flyers" built in the new shed, there was little favorable news to report about the two brothers and their "crazy experiments."

As it often happens, frequent failures lead to success. The learning curve begins when, by the process of elimination, unsuccessful methods are tossed aside, opening up the pathway to the ones that will work.

So by September 15, 1904 they were making flights up to half a mile in length, involving full turns in the air.

In another letter to Josh, Orville wrote:

"Great news! Today I flew a complete circuit of the Prairie, covering 4,080 feet in just one minute, 35 seconds."

Flights became longer in endurance and farther in distance. More commonplace was the number of accidents that occurred. In their journals, they told of "broken wings, (the pine spars shatter like taffy), smashed propellers, damaged rudders and broken supporting members." Discouraging? Certainly, but not so much that they gave up.

The many accidents, the unbelieving public, the uncooperative weather, none of these elements caused the Wright brothers to slow down. Despite what others said, they knew the airplane was flyable. That proof was behind them at Kitty Hawk.

1904, 1905, 1906, AND 1907

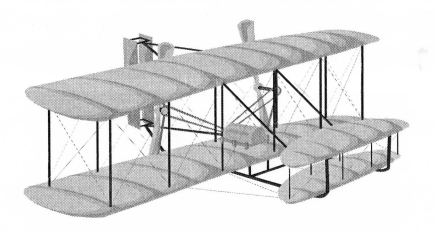

CHAPTER 21

WHAT NEXT?

The intervening years flew by: 1904, 1905, 1906, and 1907. News of the Wright's discovery of powered flight spread all over the world. Responsibilities for the inventors increased. Wilbur spent months in Europe, demonstrating the aircraft and entering competitions to prove its airworthiness.

Orville spent most of his time at the factory building airframes, and putting together more aircraft.

Their activities up to now were centered on upgrading the aircraft to sell it for military and commercial use. But their reluctance to show it, to demonstrate its abilities, hampered every effort made to sell one.

They spent almost five years in futile negotiations with the governments of the USA, Britain, Germany and France. Finally, in 1906, the U.S. Patent office granted them their long-awaited patents. This, they hoped, would protect them against the ever-increasing numbers of experimenters actively engaged in stealing their ideas.

After Josh graduated from the University, he spent a few weeks in Kitty Hawk, resting and visiting with his family. He wasn't the only one changed in the eight years since the Wright brothers came to the Outer Banks. Ezzie was nineteen years old now and Nancy was fifteen. The economy had improved by this time and the family was living in better circumstances.

Ezra followed his Dad's footsteps into the commercial fishing industry and would one day take over the family business. Nancy was still the pet of the family. Squeeker, the Calico cat had long since died.

Josh's last night was spent at home with the family. They reminisced about the days when the Wright brothers were there working on the glider. The impact of their invention was now being felt in Kitty Hawk. There was renewed national interest in this locale for the tourist trade.

Many scientists and writers made trips to Kitty Hawk just to see the place where the Wright brothers lived in their tents and rough buildings. They wanted to see Kill Devil Hill, and the place where they built the track to launch the craft. Actual eye-witnesses could always be found to relate in glowing terms: "I was there when it happened."

The Morgan family enjoyed recalling these events and speculating just how Josh would fit into the next generation of aircraft built by the Wrights.

"Ma, remember when Ms.Tate made those dresses out of the wing covering material for her girls?" asked Nancy. "I still have mine, it's too small for me now, but I want to keep it to remember the Wright brothers by."

"I remember just like it was yesterday," answered Mrs. Morgan. "I reckon we have a whole lot more good memories than bad. Even though I was just sure our Joshua was going to be mistreated or somethin.'"

At that, Jim looked over at Josh and grinned, "You know your Ma was just trying to protect you from some bad danger, don't you?"

"Oh, sure, Pa, looking back, I can certainly understand her worry. After all, we didn't know those guys or what they were up to, but I guess they fooled us all." said Josh.

He continued, "I advised the Wrights that I'm ready to go to work in their airplane factory now. So tomorrow I go to Elizabeth City to catch the train to Dayton. They said they could put me up at their house. I'll be working with them as a mechanic for a while. Some day, I hope I get to fly their machine."

CHAPTER 22

THE NEWEST MEMBER OF THE TEAM

Josh, now 22 years old, arrived in Dayton on June 1, 1907. Orville met him at the train station. The two friends spent the entire evening talking about the events of the past few years. Orville brought Josh up to date on what they were doing with the airplane company.

Wilbur was in France on a business trip. Orville explained that they were in negotiations with the French government who wanted to buy one aircraft now, but later they wanted the Wright Airplane Company to build additional planes for their military.

Other governments as well, such as Britain, Germany and Russia were also interested in discussions about acquiring aircraft for their military.

To hear them tell about it, this new attention to their achievements took all of their time and energy, leaving little time for research and development. Reporters hounded them night and day. There seemed to be a never-ending parade of airplane enthusiasts who were constantly asking for detailed drawings of the aircraft.

Newspaper reports bombarded them, mostly with inaccurate accounts of their experiments and trial runs. It was all the two brothers could do to keep up with the barrage of questions and requests for interviews.

This is why they were so pleased Josh was there to help Charlie Taylor in the airplane factory. With the help of family members, the two were important to the ongoing expansion of the projects.

Orville worked hard to complete five new planes, exact replicas of the 1905 flyer. The principal changes were the seating arrangement, the controls, and more powerful engines. The many flights made at the testing grounds of Huffman Prairie proved to be exhausting for the pilots who had to lie in a prone position to control the aircraft. The change in design allowed two people to fly in an upright position so new controls were installed to replace the hip cradle.

One day, Orville approached Josh about learning to fly. With all the testing that had to be done, they could use another test pilot. Josh was a natural pilot, and Orville was pleased that he could turn one more task over to him.

Josh fit right into his niche at the factory, having worked there previous summers. There was much for him to do. Assembling the parts and pieces for new airframes was the first assignment for him in his new position. This is what he had studied for at the university. This was the realization of his dreams.

Meanwhile, Orville worked practically non-stop to prepare a prototype aircraft to be demonstrated to the U. S. Government, and to be used for military purposes. He made trips back to Kitty Hawk to run tests before the plane's completion. Cables and letters flew across the ocean between Wilbur and Orville to keep each other posted about this new plane, and other business matters. Josh, in the meantime, kept the shop going so production would stay at the highest level.

CHAPTER 23

THE FRENCH CONNECTION

It seemed odd to Josh that even though their achievement at Kitty Hawk was a documented success, they had failed so far to convince the U.S. government of the value of their invention.

The Wright brothers then turned their attention to France. Many contacts were made with various members of the French government. After many years of intense negotiations, Wilbur was finally invited to demonstrate their flying machine.

His demonstrations of powered flight were enthusiastically received by the public and the press of France. The crowds attending them grew larger by the day. The word was out. The Wrights' "airplane fever" was sweeping the continent.

The London Daily Mirror had reporters on the scene. Headlines read, "The most wonderful flying machine that has been made. Wilbur Wright is proving over and over that they have mastered the art of actual flight. They are a public justification of the performances which the American aviators announced in 1904 and 1905, and they give them, conclusively, first place in the history of flying machines."

The Italian newspaper, Le Figaro, was even more colorful, "I've seen him; I've seen them! Yes, I have today seen Wilbur Wright and his great white bird, the beautiful mechanical bird. There is no doubt! Wilbur and Orville Wright have well and truly flown."

This was, indeed, the moment when the Wright brothers became international celebrities.

Yet, even now with proof positive that the airplane was all they said it was, the French syndicate and the French government were being difficult to deal with.

Wilbur wrote to Josh, "Dealing with the French regarding their purchase of an aircraft from us has been frustrating to say the least. It has been difficult to keep up their confidence in our product. Even though we go out every fair day, there are still some skeptics to whom we must exhibit the airplane."

Many more months went by without a contract between the Wright Brothers and the French government. At this point, Wilbur and Orville moved ahead with their negotiations with Germany, Britain and Russia.

CHAPTER 24

MOVING ON UP

Josh and Charlie Taylor worked around the clock to assemble parts for the aircraft Orville was going to demonstrate to the Signal Corps at Fort Myer, Virginia. They had measured, cut and crated wood for the spars. Two extra engines were partially assembled, as well as spare cylinders, pistons, valves and camshafts.

Charlie had traveled ahead to supervise the uncrating and assembly of the machine in a large balloon hangar on the grounds. Josh was left in charge of the production line. Even though he was chomping at the bit to help with the demonstration at Fort Myer, he agreed his time and expertise were better used at the Wright Airplane Company in Dayton.

Orville, upon arrival, found all the materials in the shipping crates to be in perfect condition, making the assembly of the machine go smoothly.

Many notable military personnel and politicians were present at this, another historic flight at Fort Myer, Virginia. Of all the trial judges, Lieutenant Benjamin D. Foulois became a favorite of Orville.

After many successful flight demonstrations during the course of the trial runs, suddenly, a terrible tragedy occurred. Lieutenant Thomas Selfridge was taking his turn as a passenger in the aircraft Orville was piloting when something snapped. A later investigation proved it was one of the propellers that cut a guy wire, causing the airplane to crash in a heap of shattered and badly damaged pieces. Orville suffered a broken thigh, injured back, broken ribs, plus other superficial wounds. Lieutenant Selfridge did not survive the crash. This was the first recorded fatality in American aviation.

Although it was, unquestionably, a catastrophic event in their lives, the Wrights took it in stride. They immediately began to make alternative plans. Orville would recuperate in Dayton; Wilbur would continue his demonstrations and negotiating efforts in Europe. The airplane company had lost some ground, but they were determined to regain it.

While Orville healed at home, he marveled at the successes Wilbur was experiencing in France. Wilbur broke his own altitude and distance records on a regular basis. Prizes of 5,000 francs and more were his for the taking. Perhaps one of the more remarkable reports about Wilbur's success in Europe was that not only did he have the press eating out of his hand, but princes, kings and queens came from far away to see his flying demonstrations in the airplane. Wilbur happily accommodated those who asked for courtesy rides.

At last, accolades were being showered on the Wright brothers for their successes. The praises didn't faze them. Still, it helped them to realize that the world had finally acknowledged their achievement.

Phyllis R. Moses

1909

CHAPTER 25

ANOTHER TRY AT FORT MYER

After a full year in Europe, Wilbur negotiated several contracts with other countries who wanted to buy airplanes from their company. Orville's accident had interrupted the trial runs for the U.S.Army, postponing that event until his recovery. Wilbur returned home in May from his successful, but lengthy stay in Europe.

In June, 1909 Wilbur, Orville and Josh went to Fort Myer to assemble the airplane shipped there in crates for the re-scheduled trials. All went well. Orville made his first flight June 28th. They finished the trials on July 30th. Lieutenant Foulois accompanied him on the first cross-country airplane trip, a total distance of ten miles to Alexandria, Virginia and return.

The U.S. Signal Corps accepted the airplane on August 2, 1909. Because the craft had exceeded the speed guaranteed by the contract, there was a $5,000 bonus paid for the aircraft. Altogether the cost to the United States government for their first plane was $30,000.

CHAPTER 26

THE FIRST FLIGHT TRAINING SCHOOL

The contract executed between the Wright Airplane Company and the U.S. Signal Corps provided that a class of trainees would receive flight instruction. The class of pilot/officers consisted of Lieutenants Frank P. Lahm, Frederic E. Humphreys, and Lieutenant Benjamin D. Foulois. The training went well. Josh provided ground school instruction for the class. He put together instruction manuals, weather data reports and graphs, some basic navigational charts, and engine maintenance manuals for them. Wilbur was their flight instructor.

Josh wrote his parents, telling them about all the new activities.

"My next trip will be to Texas where Lieutenant Benjamin Foulois will be taking delivery on the first aircraft sold to the U.S. Army. It will be disassembled, and shipped to San Antonio, Texas. I will meet the shipment there, and with Lt. Foulois' help, reassemble it. We will demonstrate its capabilities and train pilots to fly it."

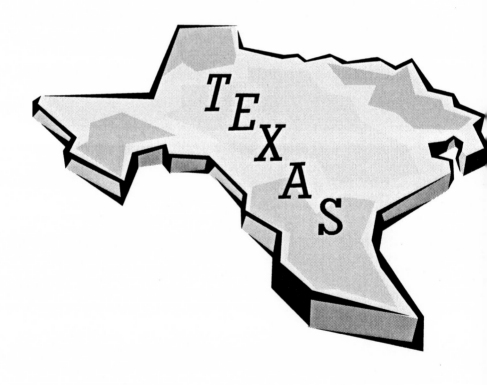

CHAPTER 27

DEEP IN THE HEART OF TEXAS

"Old Number One, as it was called, weighed 1,000 pounds. It was equipped with skids and a four-cylinder, 25-horsepower engine that "cut out" occasionally while in flight. Because it was made with skids, it could only become airborne by means of a launching rail and a catapult tower.

Lieutenant Foulois was a small man. He didn't weigh over 130 pounds. Although he was trained at Ft. Myer on the basics of flying the Wright Flyer, he had not soloed. As he put it one day, "The first day I flew Old Number One made history. It was my solo flight, my first take-off alone, my first landing, and my first crack-up. I received a few bruises and a deflated ego. We hauled the wreckage back to the hangar. We sat around trying to figure out what I did wrong in the landing.

"About a week later, I again made four flights. On the last landing, as I cut the engine, the nose went down. The airplane landed hard, which catapulted me completely out of my seat, causing me to hit my head on the structure above me. I landed a couple of feet from the seat where I should have been.

"I had the soldiers from the cavalry make me a set of leather straps which I used to secure me to the seat. From then on, this new seat belt arrangement kept me from getting bruised and banged up." Lt. Foulois became the first aviator to implement the use of safety belts.

Eventually, Lt. Foulois not only became proficient in the Army's first aircraft, but later advanced to the rank of Major General, and became Chief of the Army Air Corps.

Josh remained in San Antonio, helping Lt. Foulois until he was confident that everything was under control. When he returned to Dayton, he entertained the Wrights with humorous stories about his adventures with Lt. Foulois in Texas.

1932

CHAPTER 28

THE FINAL CHAPTER

From the first flight, Josh Morgan was one of the most important members of the Wrights' team.

His first-hand knowledge was helpful in the production and promotion of the aircraft for commercial and military use. After the sale of the Wright Aircraft Company in 1915, Josh was asked to stay on as advisor and consultant to the new owners.

The Wrights went through years of litigation because corrupt people wanted to benefit from their efforts. They dealt with charlatans and greed-driven men on a regular basis. It took an enormous amount of emotional and physical energy to take care of the many details, and the years of court appearances necessary to defend their patents.

After Wilbur's lingering illness and death in 1912, Orville carried the burdens of the wealth and fame alone. The final outcome of the search for significance in flight was the dawning of the aviation industry. They had conquered the air. They had reached goals of gigantic proportions, and had added a new dimension to the movement of man. Their loyal protégé and friend, Josh, was with them through it all.

Because of his tenure with the Wright Airplane company and the association with the Wright brothers, Josh had become an official spokesman for the miracle at Kitty Hawk. Newspaper reporters and journalists from all over hounded him constantly for interviews.

There were many monuments raised in honor of the shy, humble brothers from the Midwest. In 1920, a spectacular tribute was unveiled at Le Mans, France, in recognition of Wilbur's successes there. Monuments began to appear everywhere.

However, all monuments paled in comparison to the grand memorial at Kill Devil Hills, North Carolina. At the dedication November 19, 1932, giants of industry, military and civilian aviation greats, family and friends from all over the world were there for the ceremony.

In addition to many celebrity guest speakers, there were politicians and royalty from Europe. Also in the audience, beaming with pride, were Josh's parents, Jim and Etta May Morgan. Seated among the dignitaries, were Ezra, Nancy and their families, also invited guests. Many of their former neighbors and friends, who remembered the magical moment when powered flight was achieved, came to cheer, to pay tribute and to admire Orville, who was in his 62nd year.

Josh, now forty-seven years old, sat in the VIP section at the ceremony. He was proud of the accomplishments of the Wright brothers. Of course, some of that pride was his to claim. After the ceremony, reporters from out-of-town newspapers swarmed around Orville. He reached up and placed his hand on Josh's shoulders.

"This man, Joshua Morgan, was part of our original team. He and other residents of Kitty Hawk helped us with the earlier gliders. Then when our first powered machine came along, his part in its development was highly significant."

As one journalist wrote, "Mr. Morgan, native son of Kitty Hawk, met with us to give us his personal memories of the miracle of flight."

"Mr. Morgan then said, 'My employment with the Wright Airplane Company has been the realization of a dream. Keeping up with aviation technology and production is a challenge, to be sure. But the opportunity afforded me by the Wright brothers to be a part of this miracle is beyond words to describe.'"

As Josh looked out across the sand dunes, his gaze fell on the original camp site, not far from the Memorial. His train of thought seemed to be broken, interrupted perhaps by a picture of an excited school boy shivering in that cold December wind, running alongside a glider with its clattering engine, yelling above the noise, "We're flying the plane, we're doing it. I knew we could."

The reporter broke into Josh's thoughts, "Mr. Morgan, I understand the town of Kitty Hawk honored you earlier this year as their hometown hero. Can you describe the feelings you have about this honor?"

"I'd be happy to. It was sincere and straight from the hearts of my hometown friends here at Kitty Hawk. I lived away from here when I worked in Dayton at the airplane factory. I'm proud of this great state, North Carolina, who recognized the miracle that happened here as well as those who produced the miracle, the Wright brothers."

"Is there anything else you'd like to say, Mr. Morgan?"

Josh recalled, "Yes, I remember once at a meeting, Mr. Wilbur said,"

'If you are looking for perfect safety, you will do well to sit on a fence and watch the birds. But if you really wish to learn, you must mount the machine and become acquainted with its tricks by actual trial.'

At that moment, a flock of seagulls swooped down, diving and swirling about. As Josh watched, he remembered the words of Mr. Wilbur, "Watch the birds in their flight. You'll learn more about flying from that than anything else."

"I would like to say a few words to the young people. It is wise to learn from former generations, especially the two young men who came to our island with just their dreams. Never have two men taken their ambitions to such a height. They found their work enjoyable, no matter how discouraged they became. For them the joy of living lay in the pursuit of their ambitions. The fact that aviation has affected so many millions of people all over the globe proves their motives were praiseworthy."

"The legacy they left me was to reach beyond my imagination. To realize that with a dream to strive for, I, a humble country boy from North Carolina, could be a part of a team that designed, manufactured and flew airplanes."

"I encourage young people to see themselves in different, perhaps thrilling roles. Become a part of an inquiring society. There are folks who will be happy to help you realize your dreams. Who knows? Maybe you will be one whose immortal discovery changes the world."

"Flying sets you free. The airplane represents freedom, joy and delight. Just watch the birds, you'll understand."

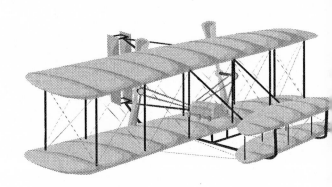

"Hold fast to dreams, for if dreams die, Life is just a broken-winged bird that cannot fly." ~*Langston Hughes*

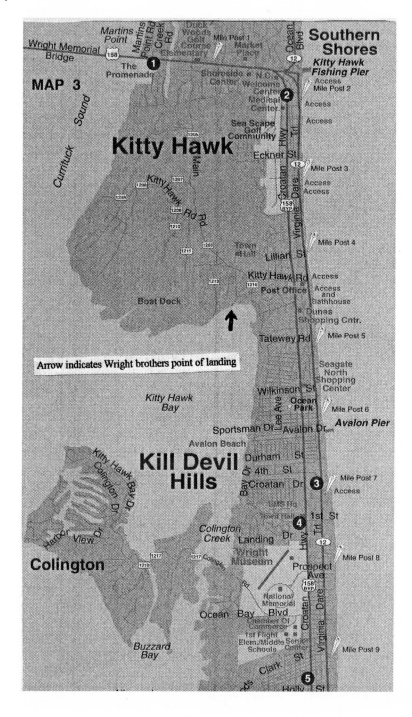

Arrow indicates Wright brothers point of landing

About the Author

Phyllis, native of Ft. Worth, Texas, now living in Georgetown, Texas, is a freelance writer, specializing in aviation and aviation history. Her articles appear in *Woman Pilot* magazine, *General Aviation News* and *FLYER* newspaper, *Vintage Airplane*, *Flight Journal*, *Women in Aviation*, *International and Aviation Buyer's Digest*, as well as local and regional periodicals.

Married to Brian Moses, retired corporate pilot, she maintains several affiliations with aviation-related organizations, which include the Texas Chapter Antique Airplane Association; Frontiers of Flight museum; The Jimmy Doolittle Squadron, Special Aviation History Collection, University of Texas at Dallas; Experimental Aircraft Association and the Sun City Aviation Club. They own a Cessna 172 and a Piper Vagabond.

She has one son, two grandchildren, and three great-grandchildren. Phyllis' interests extend to art and music, traveling, and writing. The world of aviation has always fascinated Phyllis. She spends much of her time studying its history from the myths and legends up to the modern space age. She finds the most interesting part of this research the early pioneers who had the visions and dreams. Their persistence led the way to modern technology that made aviation what it is today. Contact the author at phylmoses@msn.com.

Printed in the United States
16867LVS00001B/174

9 781410 719201